AF383181

BECOMING HUMAN

Becoming Human

Meditations on Christian Anthropology in Word and Image

JOHN
BEHR

designed by Amber Schley Iragui

ST VLADIMIR'S SEMINARY PRESS
CRESTWOOD NEW YORK 2013

LIBRARY OF CONGRESS CATALOGING-IN-PUBLICATION DATA

Behr, John.
  Becoming human / John Behr.
      p. cm.
  Includes bibliographical references.
  ISBN 978-0-88141-439-4
1. Theological anthropology—Christianity. 2. Human beings.
3. Jesus Christ—Person and offices. I. Title.
  BT701.3.B44 2012
  233—dc23

                                                        2012033332

copyright © 2013 by John Behr
ST VLADIMIR'S SEMINARY PRESS
575 Scarsdale Road, Yonkers, New York 10707
1-800-204-2665 • www.svspress.com

ISBN 978-0-88141-439-4

Typeset in Minion, Humanistika, Dear Sarah, and Scala Sans.

 for the Three Behrs

Contents

Foreword

This book reflects upon various dimensions and implications of the astounding fact that Christ shows us what it is to be God by the way he dies as a human being and, in so doing, simultaneously shows us what it is to be a human being, freely choosing to ground our life and existence in the self-sacrificial love that is God's.

These reflections are presented and
developed through word and image,
the interplay between them enriching
and deepening our understanding and
appreciation of the wisdom of God
deployed in creation, in salvation, in
ourselves. The layout of the text reflects
the movement of thought unfolded in the
sentences, with some words and quotations
emphasized visually by means of a different and larger font. The continuous text
of each chapter, moreover, is comple-
mented by offset quotations, in a different
color, and images, echoing or elucidating
aspects of the reflection.

The result is much like a medieval
manuscript, inclining the reader towards
a meditative reading, weighing, rather
than skimming, each word and image.

To avoid unnecessary detail on the page,
neither footnotes nor endnotes have been
used; references for images and quotations,
apart from Scripture, are given at the end
of the book according to the page on which
they appear.

"I shall become a Human Being"

"The glory of God is a living human being." St Irenaeus of Lyons wrote these beautiful and often quoted words at the end of the second century.

In his youth, he had known St Polycarp of Smyrna, who in turn had known the Apostle John.

They are remarkable words indeed.

Yet what do they mean?

Who or what is a "living human being"?

Mosaic of man being eaten by lions (2nd century).

Going back a few years, to a period with a living memory of Christ and the apostles, St Ignatius of Antioch made a similarly striking statement.

While being taken under guard to Rome to be martyred for his faith, he wrote to the Christians in that city,

imploring them not to interfere with his coming trials or, for instance,

to try to keep him alive by bribing the authorities.

While journeying slowly but surely towards a gruesome martyrdom, he nevertheless embraces his fate with joy, exclaiming:

"It is better for me to die in Christ
Jesus than to be king over the ends of
the earth. I seek him who died for our
sake. I desire him who rose for us.
Birth-pangs are upon me. Suffer me,
my brethren; hinder me not from
living, do not wish me to die.

…Suffer me to receive the pure light;
when I shall have arrived there, I shall
become a human being (*anthropos*).
Suffer me to follow the example of the
Passion of my God."

"Do not wish me to die"

…by finding a way to get me out of my coming
   martyrdom!

"Do not hinder me from living"

…by stopping me from being martyred!

Compared to our usual patterns of speech,
life and death are here reversed.

His martyrdom is his birth,

…and it will be a birth
in which he becomes a "human being"
—a human being in the stature of Christ,
the "perfect human being"

or the "new human being,"
as the martyr refers to "the faithful martyr,
the firstborn of the dead" (Rev 1.5),
"the Pioneer of our salvation" (Heb 2.10).

These are dramatic words and, as we will see,
very profound.

*Death, here, is a defining moment:
not the end, but the beginning;
not disappearance, but revelation.*

As St Ignatius also pointed out to the
Romans:

> "Now that Christ is with the
> Father, he is more visible than
> he was before."

That is, when Christ walked amongst us in
the flesh, we never really understood who he
was;
now that he has passed through his Passion
   and is with the Father,
      we finally "see" who he is.

Knowing Christ

All this is grounded in the crux, the high point, and the turning point of the Gospel accounts of Christ.

In Matthew, Mark, and Luke
(we will consider John later),
it is only through the Pascha of the Lord that
the disciples came to know who he truly is.

Despite having been with Christ for a number of years,

seeing him transfigured on Tabor and working miracles, hearing his teaching, and learning from his mother about the circumstances of his birth—despite all this, they abandon Christ at his Passion.

Relief on pulpit depicting the denial of Saint Peter (12th–14th century).

Peter even denies him!

The only exception—Peter on the road to Caesarea Philippi (Mat 16)—is the exception that proves the rule.

When asked, Peter affirms: "You are the Christ, the Son of the living God."

Pietro Cavallini (c.1250–1330), detail from fresco depicting scenes from the life of Saints Peter and Andrew.

Nonetheless, Christ points out that Peter did not know this by flesh and blood,

that is, by seeing and hearing Christ in the flesh.

It was by a revelation from the Father that Peter made his confession of faith—

Peter, the rock upon which Christ then declares that he will build his church, and that whatever Peter binds and looses, so it will be in heaven.

It is then, and only then, that Christ tells Peter—this supposed rock— that he must go to Jerusalem to suffer. Given that he has just been commended, it is perhaps understandable that Peter's reply is:

"That will never happen to you!"

Yet for this he gets the sharpest rebuke
imaginable from Christ:

"Get behind me Satan!"

"Get behind me, Satan!"

The paradox is absolute:
    the one, the only disciple to confess
    before the Passion
that Christ is the Son of God,
a few verses later is now called "Satan!"
As Christ himself uses the term,
    "Satan" would apply to anyone who
    separates Christ from the Cross.

Before the Cross, the disciples simply
    do not understand who Christ is.
But then, when they see him crucified they
don't understand either: they run in fear.
    Nor do they understand
when they discover the empty tomb—
for an empty tomb is, after all, ambiguous.
    Their reaction was to ask whether
    someone had stolen the body.

O foolish men,
and slow of heart to
believe all that the
prophets have spoken!
Was it not necessary
that the Christ should
suffer these things
and enter
into his glory?

Luke 24.25–6

Ivory plaque depicting
the encounter with
Christ on the road to
Emmaus (9th century).

And even when we come to the encounters with the risen Christ, even then the disciples do not recognize him immediately.

Each account of how they do come to recognize him has a particular point to make—that is, a point *for us*.

One of the most important and familiar
is the encounter with Christ
    on the road to Emmaus (Lk 24).
When the Risen Christ joins the disciples walking on the road,
    they do not recognize him.

It has only been a few days and yet
they do not recognize him.
In fact, they even start telling this "stranger"
all that had happened and how some of their
group had found the tomb empty
…They still don't get it!

*Clearly, a point
    is being made here.*

The Risen Lord then opens the Scriptures to
show how Moses and all the Prophets had
spoken of how the Christ had to suffer to
enter into his glory.
Only then do their hearts start to soften,
and after persuading him to stay the night,
their eyes were finally opened
with the breaking of the bread.

*However, at this point,
he disappears from sight!*

His disciples did not understand this at first; but when Jesus was glorified, then they remembered that this had been written of him and had been done to him.

John 12.16

Once they finally recognize him,
finally know him
    —the crucified and exalted Lord—
    to be the Son of God,
            he passes from their view.

Hence, from the beginning, Christians have been waiting for his coming. The earliest Christian writings that now comprise the New Testament do not speak of a "second coming," but instead describe more simply and directly how Christians await the coming of their Lord.

Christ was, is, and always remains the "coming one"—

            whose coming,
            whose presence,
            whose parousia,
            coincides with
                his passage,
                his transitus,
                his exodus

—leaving us a trace of his presence
and igniting a desire for him.

As St Augustine wrote in his *Confessions*:

"Through him you sought us when we were not seeking you, but you sought us that we might begin to seek you."

Considering how it is that the disciples come
to know Christ is important for two reasons.

THREE

"Moses wrote of Me"

First, it means that there is no historical distance at all between those disciples back then and us. We are not at a disadvantage by not "being there" two thousand years ago.

"Being there" did not help the disciples, and we delude ourselves if we think that we would have known better.

In fact, in so doing, we place ourselves in the category of the demonically possessed,
>   for they have no trouble
>   recognizing Christ.

By thinking we would have known Christ prior to Pascha, we would also deserve the rebuke given to Peter for having separated Christ from the Cross.

No.

The disciples came to know Christ as the crucified and risen Lord who, himself, opens the Scriptures and breaks the bread.

It is exactly this that now happens in the Church.

> *In the Church, we are still on the road to Emmaus.*

"You search the Scriptures because you think that in them you have eternal life; yet it is they that bear witness to me."

John 5.39

In the Church, the Scriptures are opened
to us—in the readings, the preaching,
the hymnography, the iconography,
the liturgical rites.
And in the midst of all this,
bread is broken in the eucharistic
offering,

and we become his body.

Fresco of the
Last Supper
(12th century).

The conversion of the Apostle Paul provides a vivid example of the approach to Scripture used in the Church thereafter.

He had studied the Scriptures
as a young man;
He had trained in various rabbinic interpretations.

> Yet he did not "see" Christ in the Scriptures, nor recognize Christ in those whom he was persecuting.

In fact, on the basis of his reading of Scripture, he regarded himself as

> *"blameless before the law,"*

and so zealous in his righteousness that he persecuted the Christians as obvious blasphemers (Phil 3.4–6).

Before the sojourn of Christ, the Law and the Prophets did not contain the proclamation which belongs to the definition of the Gospel, since he who explained the mysteries in them had not yet come. But since the Savior has come and has caused the Gospel to be embodied, he has by the Gospel made all things as Gospel.

– Origen

However, once he encountered Christ
on the road to Damascus—
with the directly challenging words,

"Why are you persecuting me?"

(Acts 22.7–8)

—he began to read the Scriptures anew,
to see in them how they had always spoken
about the Passion of Christ
and about our need for salvation.
The text had not changed; his starting point
or "first principle" had changed.

Instead of attempting to understand what
the text might have originally "meant,"
the task now becomes
what it "means" today,
as addressed to the hearers, presenting
Christ knocking at the door of their hearts,
wanting to make his abode therein.

This also means that the inspiration of the
writers of Scripture cannot be separated

from the inspired reading of Scripture, for both are revealed and enabled only by the act of the Lord, the slain Lamb, opening the book (Rev 5.9)!

From an illuminated manuscript of Beatus of Liébana, *Commentary on the Apocalypse*: The vision of the Lamb surrounded by evangelists and elders (c.950).

Destroying Death by Death

The second point is that it is by his death that Christ conquers death, revealing life everlasting.

This is of such paramount importance that one risks using too many words to emphasize it. Or rather, it has such awesome implications that one is, in fact, lost for words.

Christ does not show himself to be God by being "almighty," as we tend to think of this—

　　　　as moving mountains, throwing lightening bolts and so on—

　　　　　　　　it is rather by the *all-too-human* act of dying, in the particular manner that *he* does.

Death is, in point of fact, the only thing that all men and women have in common from the beginning of the world onwards, throughout all regions and cultures of the world.

And thus Christ reveals what it is to be God through the only thing that we have in common. He does this not simply by dying—for that would merely have been a capitulation of God, the end—

rather, he does it by the way that he has died.

Crucifixion,
Ohrid School
(13th century).

Had Christ revealed what it is to
be God in any other way—

    for example, by being rich
and powerful (reflecting our own
desires),

    or poor and an outcast
(as we might conclude by hearing
prophetic and evangelical injunc-
tions),

    or by being a first-century
Jewish male (in a quest for the
"historical Jesus")—

    any such option would
have excluded some people:
for those who do not fit any such
group would have had no part in him.

Alternatively, if it were simply because he was
human, like us, that he died, but because he
is also God he is able to get himself out of
the grave,

    that would have been great for him,

      but would not really have helped others.

22

Such things are unworthy of any considera-
tion at all. As we will see, it is rather because
he conquers death by his death that

*he enables all men and women also
to use their own mortality to come
to life in him.*

This is the heart of the theology defended by
the councils.
That which we see in the crucified and risen
Christ, as proclaimed by the apostles through
the words drawn from Scripture—from the
prophecies and the accounts, the poetry and
the prayers—

    that is what it is to be God,
this is the heart of the faith defended in the
Councils of Nicaea and Constantinople in
the fourth century.
This is the meaning of the affirmation that
Christ is "consubstantial with the Father,"

that he is *what* it is to be God and yet *other* than the Father.

Moreover, this is only known in and through the Holy Spirit, by whom alone we are able to confess Christ as Lord (1 Cor 12.3), in whom we are also adopted as sons of God, and whom we therefore also confess to be *what* it is to be God, one of the Holy Trinity.

The heart of the definition of the Council of Chalcedon is that what it is to be human and what it is to be God

—death and life—

are seen in one concrete being (*hypostasis*), with one "face" (*prosopon*).

That is, we do not look at one being to see God and another to see man.

No! Both are revealed together

—"without confusion, change, division, separation."

Byzantine Resurrection
(9th century).

What it is to be God and what it is to be human remain the same, but the miracle is that each

is now revealed together in one
and, therefore, also through each other:
mortality is not a property of God,
creating life is not a property of humans,
but Christ has brought both together,
conquering death by his death and in this very act conferring life immortal. And, moreover, as the subsequent Councils affirm, this one is the eternal Word of God and the image of the invisible God.

FIVE

"Behold the Human Being" — "It is Finished"

The Gospel of John begins where Matthew, Mark, and Luke conclude. In their accounts, it is only at the end, by encountering the Crucified and Risen One, in the opening of the Scriptures, that the disciples finally know who Christ is.

This is the very point at which the Gospel of John begins. After the opening verses (known as the "Prologue"), the narrative begins with the Baptist crying out when he sees Jesus:

"Behold the Lamb of God" (Jn 1.29). Then, when Philip told Nathaniel,

"we have found the one of whom Moses in the law and the prophets wrote," Christ subsequently tells him,

"you will see greater things than these!"

(Jn 1.44–51)

The movement from the other Gospels to John parallels the phrase in the liturgy of St John Chrysostom:

Karapet of Altamar, manuscript illumination: Interment of Christ (15th century).

"in the night in which he was given up, no, rather, gave himself up…"

The movement from one to the other,
    from a human, historical perspective,
    to a divine, eternal perspective,
is vital for all true theology.

He committed no sin;
no guile was found
on his lips. When he
was reviled, he did
not revile in return;
when he suffered,
he did not threaten;
but he trusted to him
who judges justly.
He himself bore our
sins in his body on
the tree, that we might
die to sin and live to
righteousness

1 Peter 2.22–4

In the other Gospels, the disciples see Christ being put to death and flee in fear. Again, to drive the point home: it was not seeing the empty tomb or even meeting the risen Christ unknowingly that persuaded them. It was, rather, the opening of the Scriptures and the breaking of the bread. Only in this way did they now know that this is the one spoken of in Scripture—that he is, for instance, the Suffering Servant of whom the prophet Isaiah spoke, the one who, although no guile was found on his lips, nevertheless willingly bore our sins upon himself, silently as a lamb, going to the slaughter, to offer propitiation to God (Isa 53).

Only now do the disciples know that he went not only voluntarily to his death,
　　　　but gave himself in a total
　　　　and absolute self-offering,
for, unlike the rest of us,
　　　　death had no hold on him.

By the opening of the Scriptures and the breaking of bread, we move from "he was given up" to "he gave himself up."

This is what we see in the transition from the other Gospels to that of John. In his Gospel, John depicts Christ as the exalted Lord from the beginning. Christ repeatedly tells his disciples that he is from above

    —from the heavens,
      from the Father,

while they are from below
    —from the earth,
      from Adam.

Leaf from manuscript of Beatus of Liébana, *Commentary on the Apocalypse* (c.1180).

As such, if Christ goes to the Cross,
    he does so voluntarily, *and thus his elevation on the cross is his exaltation in glory.*

The Healing of the Blind Man
from an illuminated Gospel
(12th century).

Identified as the Lamb of God from the
beginning of the Gospel,

Christ is crucified, naturally, at the
time of the slaying of the lamb in the
temple, rather than on the following day
as in the other Gospels.

And his crucifixion
is now depicted differently:
he is not abandoned, for his mother and
beloved disciple are there,
and his words are not the cry of
abandonment as in the other Gospels,
where there is no answer,
so that our attention is relentlessly focused
on the Crucified One as the Word of God.

Rather, after addressing his mother and
beloved disciple with words we will consider
later, Christ says with stately majesty:

"It is finished,"

and he "hands over the Spirit" (Jn 19.30).

What is finished?

Is it the work of God that is finished?

But what is this?

An account of healing told only in John might give us a clue.

The blind man healed by Christ was born blind not because of his fault or that of his parents but, as Christ says,

"in order that the works of God might be made manifest."

(Jn 9.3)

St Irenaeus points out that the way Christ then heals the blind man, by mixing spit and earth, parallels our initial fashioning, the mixing of the power of God with the dust of the earth. So St Irenaeus concludes,

> "The work of God is the
> fashioning of the human being."

Cupola mosaic of scenes from Genesis (13th century).

We are back to *the human being*.

What is a "human being"
　　　—the handiwork that God
　　　　devotes himself to?

For an answer, we must, of course, turn
back to Genesis. When we do, we find a
striking difference in the way that God's
activity is described in its opening chapter.

　　　Scripture begins with God
　　　　issuing commands:

Let there be light—and there was light.

Let there be a firmament …

Let the waters under the heavens be gathered …

Let the earth put forth vegetation …

Let there be light in the firmament …

Let water bring forth swarms of living creatures …

Let the earth bring forth living creatures …

This divine "fiat"—"Let it Be"—

is sufficient to bring all these creatures into
existence:

"and it was so … and it was good."

Having declared all these things into
existence by a word alone, God then
announces his own project—not with
an injunction but in the subjunctive:

*"Let us make the human being
(anthropos) in our image,
after our likeness."* (Gen 1.26)

This is the work of God.
This is what he has set his mind to.
This is what he specifically deliberates about.
This is the divine purpose and resolve.

And this is the only thing that is *not* followed
by the words "and it was so."

*This project of God,
God's own work, is not
completed by his word alone.*

In fact, God does not even simply and
solely make a human being (*anthropos*) at
that point;

> instead he makes males and females…

Only with the culmination of all theology in
the Gospel of John do we hear that the work
of God is complete. Shortly before Christ
declares that it is "finished," we hear confir-
mation of the completion of God's project
in the words uttered unwittingly by Pilate:

> "Behold the human being" (Jn 19.5).

Christ, over whom death had no claim so
that he genuinely went voluntarily to his
death, conquering death by his death, is the
first true human being in history. He *is* the
image of the invisible God (Col 1.15).

It was for the new human being that human nature was created at the beginning, and for him mind and desire were prepared.... It was not the old Adam who was the model for the new, but the new Adam for the old.... For those who have known him first, the old Adam is the archetype because of our fallen nature. But for him who sees all things before they exist, the first Adam is the imitation of the second....

The work of God is complete, and the Lord of creation now rests from his work in the tomb on the blessed Sabbath.

"Moses the great mystically prefigured this present day, saying: 'And God blessed the seventh day.' For this is the blessed Sabbath, this is the day of rest, on which the only-begotten Son of God rested from all his works; through the economy of death he kept the Sabbath in the flesh, and returning again through the resurrection he has granted us eternal life, for he alone is good and loves humankind (literally: loves *anthropos*)."

–Vespers of
Holy Saturday

This hymn does not compare Christ's "rest" after his Passion with the "rest" of God back in time immemorial.

Instead, it makes an absolute identification. It does not say:

as he rested back then, so he is now resting again. It says, instead:

This is the blessed Sabbath.

This is a very concrete example of how there is no historical distance at all in the liturgical celebration of the Church. And more, the work of God is completed in the present, as will be discussed below.

The project, the work of God announced at the beginning is completed at the end by one who is God. As St Maximus put it:

Christ, as human, completes what he himself, as God, has predetermined to take place.

Detail of the dead Christ
from a Byzantine Epitaphios
(14th century).

If this is the case,
then we have yet to become human—
and, as St Ignatius testifies so resoundingly,
we only and finally do so by following Christ
through our own *martyria*,
our own witness and
confession of him.

And finally... according to
the concept of humanity, he
goes to God himself, having
"appeared on our behalf,"
clearly, as it is written, "in
the presence of the God" and
Father, as anthropos—the
one who as Word cannot be
separated in any way at all
from the Father—fulfilling
as anthropos, in deed and
truth, with unchangeable
obedience, everything that he,
as God, has predetermined to
take place, and accomplishing
the whole will of the God
and Father on our behalf.

-St Maximus the Confessor,
referring to Heb 9.24

SIX

The Paradox of Death

Clearly then, a lot revolves around death, and how one understands death depends upon how one perceives it.

As a biological event, death is unavoidable and simply a matter of fact: all things that come to be in time will pass in time.

We were born without any choice on our
part. Through an act of procreation between
a male and a female, we have each been cast
into existence—moreover, an existence in
which whatever we do we will die.

    However "good" we try to become,
      we assuredly will die
—again, without any choice on our part.

So much for freedom and free will!

In fact, death is the only unavoidable part
of life.
It is the only thing which I can be sure of,
    and, thus,
the only thing which I must contemplate.
Death is a necessity in my life,
    as my life is a given for me.

However, as we begin to reflect on the fact
of death in the light of Christ's triumph over

death, we can begin to see further aspects to this, making the transition from a human to a divine perspective.

The first is that death is, in fact, tragic.

This is, of course, a natural reaction.
Yet why it should be so,
and not simply a neutral fact,
> is really only understood in the
> light of Christ.

Prior to the coming of Christ, there was no real sense in the Old Testament that death itself is tragic;
> death, as we said above,
> > is a matter of fact.
Violent death, death at the hands of the ungodly and wicked is certainly tragic.
> But death in the fullness of ripe old
> age, with family around, in peace,

and with a proper burial was
    held to be natural, right and proper.

Now, however, in light of Christ's victory
over death, death is revealed to be
"the last enemy" (1 Cor 15.26).
We can now understand that men and
women don't simply die as a neutral,
biological fact;
        they die by having turned
        away from their Creator,
        their only source of life.

Our turning away, our apostasy, our falling
into death is not simply something that
happened at the beginning of time—
                someone else's fault!

It is something that each of us struggles with
constantly in this life.
        We are constantly tempted, as Adam
was at the beginning, to think that we are actually sufficient unto ourselves, that we have
life in ourselves—

Hildegard of Bingen, Left:
Prophets and Patriarchs; Right:
Apostles and Martyrs (1151).

43

Saint Sisoes the Great
before the tomb of
Alexander the Great
(20th century, based on
Byzantine fresco).
The text reads:

*Sisoes, the great among
the ascetics, stood before
the tomb of Alexander,
Emperor of the Greeks,
who at one time had
shone with glory; and
horrified by the inexorable
passing of time and the
vanity of the transient
world, "Lo!" he cried
aloud, "Beholding thee,
O grave, I fear the
judgement of God and
I weep, for the common
destiny of all mankind
comes to mind!
O death, who
can escape thee?"*

—that the life *I* have is my own,
    to do with as *I* please,
and that should *I* perhaps feel *I* want
    to be "good" or "religious,"
I can do so by doing something charitable
for my neighbor
    (as long as it doesn't threaten my own
    stability and well-being),
or by allocating *some* time to God
    (on Sunday, perhaps, for I don't want
    to be a fanatic after all!).
Yet living this way, eventually and certainly
we will find out that however "good" or
"religious" we make ourselves,
        we will still die,
        returning again to the earth as dust.

However, if we take our reflection one step
further, in the light of Christ, we can see
even greater profundity in the depths of the
wisdom and the providence of God.

−Deut 32.39

Christ's work is not simply an *ad hoc* measure in response to a man-made problem.

Rather, just as it is the starting point for understanding the tragic dimension of death, so, too, is it the starting point for understanding the overarching work of God.

Death is indeed the catastrophe that happens when the creature turns his back on the Creator,

the source of life. Yet, Christ's own work has turned death inside-out, showing himself to be stronger than death,

and proving himself to be the one who is ultimately and totally in control from the beginning:

All things are in his hands and providence—even our apostasy. Turned inside-out, death now becomes the means whereby the creature returns to God,

and, in fact, is fashioned by God as a living
human being.

The full scope of what we considered earlier—that Christ destroyed death by his death—now comes to light.

It was by his death—
that most human of
actions, and the only
thing that we have in
common from the
beginning of the
world onwards, and
an action which
expresses all the
weakness and the
impotence of our
created nature—
by this, and nothing less,
has Christ shown himself
to be God.

"I weep and I wail when I think upon death, and behold our beauty, fashioned after the image of God, lying in the tomb, disfigured, dishonored, bereft of form. O marvel! What is this mystery which befalls us? Why have we been given over unto corruption, and why have we been wedded to death? Of a truth, as it is written, by the command of God, who gives the departed rest."

–St John of Damascus

In so doing, and without minimizing the tragedy of death, Christ has opened up a way of seeing a deeper mystery in death and has transformed death throughout all time:

> for what was once the end,
> now becomes the beginning
> of a deeper mystery.

Fiat! Let it Be!

As it is through his death that he conquered death, Christ has changed the "use" of death for all men and women throughout time.

As St Maximus the Confessor put it,

> "When willingly submitting to the condemnation imposed on our passibility [that is, our passive subjection to suffering], he turned that very passibility

into an instrument for eradicat-
ing sin and the death which is
its consequence."

Christ has provided,
as St Maximus explains,

"another beginning
and a second birth
(*genesis*) for human
nature, which
through the vehicle
of suffering, ends in
the pleasure of the
life to come."

Pieter Bruegel,
"The Land of Cockaigne"
("The Land of Plenty"),
(1566).

St Maximus says that by reaching out for
pleasure without undergoing any prior labor
or suffering, Adam introduced a form of
pleasure that, in fact, culminates in pain:
eating for the sake of the pleasure
of eating leads to gluttony,
an addiction to eating which produces pain
when one can't soothe oneself
by eating;

50

and, likewise, for all our other supposed
"pleasures."

> *Yet this is a pain which is also
> educational, for it prompts
> us to reconsider how
> we relate to pleasure.*

On the other hand, by voluntarily undergoing the Passion, the suffering of death—
    a death to which he was not liable,
    for no sin was to be found in him—
Christ has turned this vicious cycle inside-
out, making death the beginning of new life.

As St Maximus puts it:

> "Death, once it has ceased having
> pleasure as its birth-mother—
> that pleasure for which death itself
> became the natural punishment—
> clearly becomes the father
> of everlasting life."

In this way, St Maximus continues, Christ
has "converted the use of death," so that

> "the baptized acquires the use
> of death to condemn sin,
> which in turn mystically leads
> that person to divine and
> unending life."

Rather than being
passive and frustrated,
victims of death
and of the givenness
of our mortality,
in Christ we can freely
and actively
"use death,"
in St Maximus' striking phrase.

And in so doing, we will transcend
the limitations of the life into which
we have been born,
in which we have found ourselves
through no choice of our own—

Coptic Resurrection
(14th century).

the "existence" in which, whatever we do,
                              we die.

In and through Christ, we now have the
possibility of freely using the givenness of
our mortality to be reborn, by choice,
      so coming to be in a life without end.

*Only now does freedom
      —not necessity—
become the basis for a truly human
            existence in Christ.*

This is a new existence,
beginning with an act of freedom—
      that of Christ voluntarily
      going to his Passion,
      "converting the use of death" for all.

And in this way,
>   he enables us also to start over
>   *—freely—*
>   by following him.

This begins sacramentally, once and for all in baptism,
>   where the baptized commit themselves to dying to Adam
>   and to living in Christ, being
>   "born from above… from the
>   water and the Spirit" (Jn 3.3, 5).

And it is continued or renewed, thereafter, throughout the whole of life by "taking up the cross and following" Christ (Mat 16.24).

This baptismal life is nourished by the Body and the Blood of Christ himself,
>   continuing to participate in the
>   broken bread, with the disciples
>   on the road to Emmaus,
and in so doing, "proclaiming his death until he comes" (1 Cor 11.26).

And, as Adam was "a
type of the one to come"
(Rom 5.14),
      the breath of life
which animated Adam
prefigures the gift of
the Spirit given to the
baptized as a pledge,
      a first taste of
the fullness of the life-
creating power of the
Spirit,
      already rendering
Christians spiritual,
even now,
      as they begin to put to death the
desires of the flesh and to begin, instead,
to live in the gifts of the Spirit:

      love, joy, peace, patience, kindness,
      goodness, faithfulness, gentleness,
      and self-control (Gal 5.22–3).

Detail from Romanesque
painted ceiling depicting
the Baptism of Jesus
(c.1150).

*This new "use of death"
is not an act of desperation
bringing about the end,*

or an act of
passive submission to victimization,
resigning oneself to one's fate.

It is, rather, the beginning of new life for
the baptized and for those around them,
a new mode of existence
   —"in Christ" rather than "in Adam"—
manifest in the baptized.

Yet it is so only to the extent that they
actively take up the cross,
   that is, no longer live for themselves
   in an ego-centric mode of life,
     but rather live ecstatically,
      beyond themselves, for their
      neighbors and for God.

Through Christ's work, we need no longer
be passive victims of the mortality into
which we have been thrown,
         for now we can actively

"use death"

as the beginning of a new mode of life,

*a birth
into existence
as a human being.*

57

EIGHT

Learning by Experience

St Irenaeus stated that God did not create human beings "perfect" at the outset, and he offered various reasons why.

He suggested, for instance, that Adam and Eve, whom he depicts as infants in paradise, needed to grow in order to achieve perfection,

the fullness of being human to which they were called by God.

For example, a mother could give a
newborn child meat rather than milk,
though this would not
     benefit the infant at all.
Likewise, God could have given us a
full share in his life and existence
from the beginning—
     but we would not have
     been able to receive such a
     magnificent gift,

*without being
prepared by learning
     through experience.*

A newborn infant may have "perfect" limbs,
but needs to exercise (and to fall)
     before being able to walk and to run; so,
too, creatures needs to be exercised in virtue
     before they can share in
          the uncreated life of God.

He further explains that this is bound up with different kinds of "knowledge." There is a knowledge that is acquired by hearing, say, that Paris is in France;

and then there is a knowledge which is only gained by experience, such as what it is for something, such as honey, to be sweet.

Moreover, someone who has lost their sight, but then regains it will value sight much more than those who do not know what it is like to be blind.

Likewise, he suggests it is only by our mortality, by the experience of death in our separation—apostasy—from God,
that we come to value life,
knowing that in ourselves we
do not have life,
but depend for it upon God.

Our experience of death drives home this point in a way that we will never otherwise fully know:

It makes the point existentially, in the guts, rather than just in the head.

We need to know experientially what it is to be weak, if we are to know the strength of God, for as Christ both exemplified and affirms: "my strength is made perfect in weakness" (2 Cor 12.9).

St Irenaeus points to the case of Jonah as an analogy for understanding the wisdom of God in these matters. God appointed a whale to swallow up Jonah, not so as to kill him, but to provide an occasion for Jonah to learn. By being in the belly of the whale for three days and nights and then unexpectedly cast out, Jonah acknowledged himself to be a servant of the Lord who made heaven and earth.

Giotto, Fresco of Jonah and the Whale (c.1305).

61

So, likewise, St Irenaeus suggests that in preparing beforehand the plan of salvation worked by the Lord through the sign of Jonah,

God allowed the human race to be swallowed up by the great whale from the beginning.

God did so, once again, not so that the human race should perish,

but that once they received salvation, they would then know that they do not have life from or in themselves.

They would, instead, acknowledge God as the Creator and themselves as created,

depending for life and existence from God alone

and now willing to receive it.

In this providential plan, the human race
comes to learn of its own weakness,
but also and simultaneously
        comes to know the greatness of God
manifest in its own weakness,
transforming the mortal to immortality
        and the corruptible to incorruption.

Jonah is,
        therefore, a sign of
the perishing human race and,
at the same time,
        a sign of the Savior,

for it is precisely
        by his death
                that Christ has conquered death.

Finally, St Irenaeus adds that only in this way
can there be created beings
> who can freely respond to God in love,
> who can adhere to him in love,
> and so, in love,
> come to share in his existence.
Any other approach would have resulted
merely in "automatons."

He then concludes, rather shockingly,
that if we ignore all this, and especially the
need for experiential knowledge of our own
weakness:

"We kill the human being in us."

From what we have seen, we might also say
that in order to be a true human being
in the image of God,

who is Christ the true human being,
we must be born into a new existence
in Christ

by a birth effected through our
voluntary use of our mortality
—as an act of sacrifice through baptism—
thereby

*freely choosing
to exist as a human being*

and grounding that being and existence in
an act of freedom, so living the same life of
love that God himself is.

*The human being
only comes into existence by
giving their own "fiat"—*

"Let it be!"

For every other aspect of creation,
all that was needed was a simple
divine "fiat"

—"Let it be!"

But for the human being
to come into existence,

*required a
creature able to
give his or her own "fiat!"*

This is, of course,
accomplished sacramentally,
once and for all, in baptism.
The life of the baptized thereafter is one of
"learning to die,"
learning, that is, specifically to take up the
Cross of Christ.

However, until I actually die and
        lie in the grave,
I'm caught in the first-person singular.
I can only say:
        "Didn't I die well to myself today?"
It is still I who am working
        while I learn how to let go of all that
        pertains to this earth and to my self.

If, however, I can do so—
        if, that is, I can learn to let go,
        to become dispassionate and not
        attached to material possessions and
        riches, even to family and my own
        image of myself—
then, when I breathe my last,
I will be able to say in peace,

"Into thy hands I commend my spirit."

If I do not learn this, then death will
certainly be painful, separating me from all
that I love, all that I can not "take with me."

Edvard Munch, "By the Deathbed" (1896).

Death will finally reveal in which
direction my heart is oriented.

However, until that point, it is still
    I who am doing this,
    dying to myself.

When, on the other hand,
    I am finally
    returned to the dust,
    then *I* stop working.

Then, and only then,
    do *I* finally experience my
    complete and utter frailty
    and weakness.

Then, and only then,
    do *I* become clay
    (for *I* never was this),
clay fashioned by the Hands of God into
living flesh.

    And so, it is also only then that the
God whose strength is made perfect in
weakness can finally be the Creator:

taking dust from the earth which I
now am and mixing in his power,
he now, finally, fashions a true, living,
human being—

        "the glory of God."

When this happens, the act begun in
    baptism is completed,
    and so too is the Eucharist.
Those who commit their spirit to the Lord
eucharistically complete their incorporation
into Christ. St Irenaeus puts the process
leading to the Eucharist in parallel with that
leading through death to resurrection.

He suggests that
    just as the wheat and the vine receive
growth and fruitfulness from the Spirit,
    so too we receive the Eucharist;
    and as we make the fruits
into bread and wine
    so too we are made ready for the
resurrection to be effected by the Word.

Suffer me to
be eaten by the
beasts, through
whom I can attain
to God. I am God's
wheat, and I am
ground by the teeth
of wild beasts that
I may be found pure
bread of Christ.

–St Ignatius of Antioch

When you take
away their breath
they die and return
to their dust;
when you send
forth your Spirit,
THEY ARE
CREATED
and you renew the
face of the ground.
May the glory of
the Lord endure
forever and may the
Lord rejoice in
his works.

Psalm 104.29-31

Then, just as the bread and the wine receive the Word to become the Body and the Blood of Christ—the Eucharist—
so also our bodies will receive immortality and incorruptibility from the Father.

Human death is educational,
enabling us to experience
the frailty of our nature
so we may experience
the strength of God,
and through this we become a eucharistic gift to and of God.

So, also, will be completed the return on the pledge of the Spirit given to Christians in baptism.
Breathing their last breath,
they are no longer animated as
they had previously been by the
breath of life.
Rather, the pledge, which had been kindling the spark of new life,

will be set ablaze in the fullness
of the life-creating power of the
Spirit
        through our actual death
and resurrection in Christ:

    "what is sown in an ani-
    mated body is raised in a
    spiritual body" (1 Cor 15.44).

In all these ways, the stated
intention of God in the first
chapter of Genesis
—to make a human being—
            is completed.
The passage from the first
creation account to the second
—when God takes *our* dust
from the earth—

            traces *our* passage
from the givenness of our existence
        to our (re)creation
            by God through death.

From illuminated manuscript of Rabanus
Maurus, *De Universo*: The Creation of Adam
(1028).

The human being is earth
            that suffers.

–Barnabas

NINE

"Male and Female Made He Them"

God's project is to make human beings.

This is what God does and this is who God is: the *phil-anthropos*,

the lover of the human being.

Yet, as we have seen, for a human being to come into existence requires a being who can say "fiat."

If achieving the desired intention of creating

human beings in the image of God requires this lengthy preparation

and a responsive, sacrificial act from the creature being fashioned,

then perhaps further depths can also be seen in our existence as male and female.

God's intended but lengthy project is to create human beings.

> *But what he actually does,*
> *more immediately, is to create*
> *men and women,*

for they are the only beings who can learn how to say "fiat."

Being "male and female" is usually considered to be something we share with other creatures.

We unthinkingly consider being "male and female" as part of the biological, physical traits of existence that we have in common with animals.

But in the opening creation poem of Genesis, no other creature is said to be "male and female." This aspect of our existence certainly enables the species to "increase and multiply" (Gen 1.28).

Yet the other creatures are also given this same command (Gen 1.22), without being called "male and female."

Being "male and female," then, is something unique to the creature called to be human.

St Maximus differentiates
> the birth (*gennesis*)
>> resulting from biological, sexual
>> procreation between a man and
>> a woman,
> from the coming-into-being (*genesis*)
>> of the true human being.

The "human being," in the full sense that we have seen that term used, is not the result of procreation,
> just as such reproduction does not result in beings who are already "in Christ" rather than "in Adam."

It is very important, however, to make it absolutely clear that this is not because of any supposed "taint" inherent in sexual activity, no matter how "purely" engaged in.

"The children of this world marry and are given in marriage" (Lk 20.34),
> resulting in more sons and
>> daughters of Adam.

Lucas Cranach the Elder, "Adam"; opposite "Eve" (1533).

This has its own God-given role to play;
          but it is not the completion
                    of God's purpose.

For those men and women to become human requires their own voluntary action to conform themselves to Christ through baptism and to take up the cross.

Beyond the "fruit of the loins"
          —the aspect of marriage which
                    belongs to this world—
marriage also provides a context for spiritual fruit and a path to the heavenly realm.

As we have seen,
martyrdom was understood by the first Christians as a birth, in Christ,
          into true existence as a human being.

In later years,
the ascetic life of monastics and celibates was also understood as
          "martyrdom":

a martyr's struggle in the arena with the beasts, represented in the *martyrologies* as demons, was now continued by the monk in the desert struggling with the demons, depicted visually as beasts. St Anthony the Great endured daily martyrdom, according to St Athanasius, by fighting with the passions and the temptations which daily assailed him.

Likewise, the crowning of the bride and groom with martyrs' crowns in the sacrament of marriage

      indicates that marriage too is an arena in which the couple learn to become human through their faithful and ascetic witness

      —*martyria*—to Christ.

Breviary of Love, Temptation
(13th–14th century)

When Christ quotes the words in Genesis
that from the beginning God made them
male and female
    so that the two might become one
flesh (Mat 19), *he makes no*
mention whatsoever of procreation:
it is simply that the two might
    become one,

and that there is to be
no dissolution of this.

Even if Moses allowed
divorce because of the
Israelite hardness of
heart, Christ, who is
before Moses,
revokes this:
    from the beginning
    it was not so.

So absolute are Christ's words about this
that they provoke his disciples to exclaim,
        in shock,
that it is better not to get married,
        thus demonstrating their
        hardness of heart!

This is indeed a "difficult" saying
of Christ, and not all can accept it
(as the disciples have just shown!).

In fact, playing with the imagery,
Christ says that to accept
this difficult saying,
        one must be as devoted as a
        "eunuch" was thought to be
        in antiquity:
that is,
one must be faithful
to the injunction of God
        —monogamous—
to be a
        "eunuch for the kingdom of heaven."

Fresco depicting the
Meeting of Joachim
and Anna at the
Golden Gate
(16th century).

Likewise, when writing to the questioning
Corinthians (1 Cor 7), Paul asserts that
because we are created as sexual beings
and thus tempted to immorality,
    every man should have a wife and
        every woman a husband,
and that they should give
themselves to each other,
    for they are each other's body.

He states this in an amazingly
reciprocal manner, putting each on a par
with the other—
    and, again, with no
        mention of procreation.

He then continues by suggesting
that for the sake of praying, married
couples might, perhaps, by mutual consent
—and then only for a temporary season—
    abstain from sexual relations to
        devote themselves to prayer in a
        more concentrated fashion.

Yet in the same breath he adds,
      "And then come back together again."

The Apostle gives concession to married
Christians, just as Moses had also earlier
given a concession.
      However, as Christ made clear,
      it was not so from the beginning.

From the beginning, then, we have needed
concessions as we learn to grow into the
reality to which we are called.

*Marriage provides a context
in which males and females are,
quite literally, humanized.*

According to St Maximus, the attributes
of being "male" and "female" are "seen
especially in men and women."

That is, for St Maximus,
> being "male" and being "female"
> is not simply equivalent to
being a "man" and a "woman,"
but is, rather, the impassioned modes
in which we currently experience
our sexuality—
> the divisive roles laid upon us
> by society, or a means of identifying
> otherness, and thus destructive of
> our being truly human.

However, he says, through the attainment
of dispassionate virtue, such things are
transcended,
> so that men and women,
> remaining men and women,
are now equally seen to be and become
> "human beings"
> —as is Christ, in whom there is
> "neither male nor female"
> > (Gal 3.28).

82

Sexual difference, thus inscribed into
human existence, is not simply there to
perpetuate the species.

    Rather, sexual difference provides a
concrete, incarnate, and immediate
experience of otherness,

evoking the possibility
of real self-sacrifice in
ecstatic and erotic love.

To reduce the otherness of
sexual difference to a biological
    (and, as sometimes claimed, "fallen")
means of reproduction
does not do justice to the
richness of human experience,
    provided by God
as the framework for our growth into
    the stature of Christ.

TEN

"The Mother of the Living"

In the first chapter of Genesis then,
God announces his project:

to create a human being in his image.

To eventually achieve this,
he creates males and females,
the creatures called to grow into the
fullness he has in view,
a type or a rough sketch
of the one to come,
as the Apostle said (Rom 5.14).

God thus provides a framework within which that
growth can take place,
    a context for being
    "humanized."

And, as we have seen,
this is finally realized in Christ
through his death-defeating
death,
    and subsequently in
those who now "use" death,
in him, to the ultimate point
of becoming clay in his
Hands.

Through this death then,
we are brought to the second creation
account in a profound way, where God
takes the earth and fashions it into an
anthropos,
    a living human being—
    the glory of God.

Souvigny Bible, God creating Eve
from Adam's rib (12th century).

Hieronymus Bosch (c.1450–
1516), *Christ creates Eve while
Adam sleeps.*

If we turn to the second creation account, in the second chapter of Genesis, we can now see new depth in its narrative.

Taken from the side of the man
is the woman, who is led to the man
as his bride, with these words:

> "For this reason shall a man
> leave his father and mother
> and join himself to his wife"
> (Gen 2.24).

Intriguingly, these words have scarcely, if ever, been practiced in human history:
in most cultures, from the earliest
times into modern times, it is the
bride who is brought into the
husband's home and family,
and bears his name.

Not surprisingly, then, this passage was taken by the Apostle Paul as referring to Christ and the Church,

the Son who leaves his Father's side in
heaven to join his spouse (Eph 5.31–2).

Tertullian develops this insight, saying:

> "As Adam was a figure of Christ,
> Adam's sleep provided
> a shadow of the death of Christ,
>   who was to sleep a mortal slumber,
> that from the wound inflicted
> on his side might be figured the
> true Mother of the living,
>   the Church."

The Church which came from the side
of the crucified Christ—pouring out as the
blood and the water when he was pierced
(cf. Jn 19.34)— *is foreshadowed by the
formation of Eve from the side of Adam
when he was asleep,*
the sleep which foreshadowed
Christ's own sleep in death.

Now I imagine that you are not ignorant
that the living Church is the body of Christ.
For the Scripture says

"God made man male and female":
the male is Christ and the female is the Church.

And moreover, the books and the Apostles
declare that the Church belongs not to the
present, but has existed from the beginning;
for she was spiritual, as also was our Jesus,
but was made manifest in the last days that he
might save us; and the Church, which is spiritual,
was made manifest in the flesh of Christ,
showing us that if any one of us guard her
in the flesh without corruption, he shall receive
back again in the Holy Spirit.

–Clement of Rome

Yet, it is only after the "curse"
that the woman is named "Eve,"
        the mother of the living (Gen 3.20),
so indicating further depths in how human
beings come to be and pointing to the
identity of "the mother of the living."

To understand further this interplay
between creation and re-creation
        through death,
        with a new Adam and
        the Mother of the living,
we must turn to the account of the
Suffering Servant in Isaiah, and in the
words that immediately follow it:

> "Sing, O barren one, who
> did not bear; break forth into
> singing and cry aloud, you who
> have not been in travail! For the
> children of the desolate one will
> be more than the children of
> her that is married, says
> the LORD" (Isa 54.1).

89

This verse from Isaiah is taken by modern scholarship to belong to a different oracle with a different theme.

But in the liturgical tradition, the verse is read together with the description of the Suffering Servant
—and as its conclusion—

over the entombed body of the
dead Christ on Holy Friday.

The Passion of Christ concludes with joyful proclamation that the barren woman will now give birth, for as we have seen:

It is into the death of Christ that Christians are baptized as newly reborn children of God in the Church — the real Mother of the Living.

The Apostle Paul
also quotes those words
of Isaiah and refers them
to the heavenly,
free Jerusalem,
    "our mother"
    (Gal 4.26).

He also describes
himself as being
"in travail," by
preaching the Gospel
of the crucified Lord,
with his converts,
    "until Christ be
    formed in you"
    (Gal 4.19)—
until they can say,
as Paul had, that having
been crucified with Christ,
it is "no longer I who live,
but Christ lives in me"
    (Gal 2.20).

The "woman clothed with the sun"
clearly means the Church, endued
with the Father's Word, whose
brightness is above the sun....
    "She being with child,
    cries, travailing in birth
    and pained to be delivered"
means that the Church will not
cease to bear from her heart the
Word that is persecuted by the
unbelieving in the world.
    "And she brought forth,"
    he says, "a manchild, who
    is to rule all the nations,"
means that the Church continually
bears Christ, the perfect man-child
of God, who is declared to be
God and human, as she teaches
all nations.

    –Hippolytus, referring to Rev 12

Sister Joanna Reitlinger (1898–1988), the martyr Blandina and her life.

And as the Apostle affirms so clearly, it is the Christians who are, individually and collectively, "the body of Christ"
(1 Cor 12.27)
—all those who "by the one Spirit have been baptized into the one body"
(1 Cor 12.13),
calling upon God as
"Abba, Father"
(Rom 8.15; Gal 4.6).

All the elements we have been considering are brought out dramatically in the example of the martyr Blandina.

As a young slave girl— the epitome of weakness in the ancient world—she personifies Christ's words to Paul:

"My strength is
made perfect in
weakness"
(2 Cor 12.9).

She was so "weak in body"
that the others were fearful lest
she not be able to make a
good confession.
Yet,

    "she was filled with
such power that even those
who were taking turns to
torture her
in every way,
from dawn until dusk,
    were weary and beaten.
They, themselves, admitted
that they were beaten…
astonished at her endurance,
as her entire body was
mangled and broken."

The Lord testified:
"the flesh is weak," yet
"the Spirit is ready," that is,
is able to accomplish what it
wills… In this way
the martyrs bear witness
and despise death…
When the weakness of the
flesh is absorbed, it manifests
the Spirit as powerful; and
again, when the Spirit
absorbs the weakness, it
inherits the flesh for itself,
and from both of these is
made a living human being:
living, indeed, because of
the participation of the Spirit;
and human, because of the
substance of the flesh.

−St Irenaeus, quoting Mat 26.41

The Crucifixion
(8th century).

Not only is she, in her weakness, filled with divine power by her confession, but she becomes fully identified with the one whose body was broken on Golgotha:

> when hung on a stake
> in the arena,
> "she seemed to hang
> there in the form of a cross,
> and by her fervent prayer
> she aroused intense
> enthusiasm in those who
> were undergoing their ordeal,
> for in their torment with their
> physical eyes they saw in the
> person of their sister him who
> was crucified for them, that he
> might convince all who believe
> in him that all who suffer
> for Christ's sake will
> have eternal fellowship
> in the living God."

Through her suffering, Blandina becomes
identified with Christ:

     she no longer lives,
     but Christ lives in her.

This is, of course, only seen by those who
are undergoing their own ordeal with her
in the arena,

     those who have also truly

     taken up the cross.

Those looking down from the seats in the
amphitheatre would have looked upon the
spectacle quite differently, though perhaps
some were moved to reflect further on what
kind of witness she was providing.

Blandina's passage out of this world
is Christ's entry into this world
and this is again
described as a birth.

After describing her suffering, and that of another Christian called Attalus, the letter continues:

"Through their continued life the dead were made alive, and the martyrs showed favor to those who had failed to witness. And there was great joy for the Virgin Mother in receiving back alive those who she had miscarried as dead. For through them the majority of those who had denied were again brought to birth and again conceived and again brought to life and learned to confess; and now living and strengthened, they went to the judgment seat."

The Christians who turn away from making their confession are

simply dead.

Their lack of preparation
has meant that they are
stillborn children of the
Virgin Mother,
        the Church.
But now, strengthened
by the witness of others,
they also are able to go
to their death,
        and so the
        Virgin Mother
        receives them back
        alive,
finally giving birth to
living children of God.

The death of the martyr
 is their "new birth,"
and the death of the
martyr is celebrated as
their true birthday.

Manuscript illumination,
"The Virgin Orans" (9th century).

The Barren Woman becomes the Mother of the Living, the Virgin Mother,

El Greco, "The Annunciation" (c.1600).

as a result of Christ's Passion
and the preaching of the Gospel
of the Resurrected Lord.

By receiving this Gospel,
the Church is made fertile,
giving birth to
many living children of God.

The person in whom
this reality is complete is,
of course,
Mary—
the first human being to say,
in reference to Christ:

"Let it be."

It is not her womb or her breasts that
define his mother's identity, as Christ
himself asserts, but
> hearing the Word of God and
> keeping it, receiving it,
> giving it flesh (Lk 8.21, 11.27–8).

Because Mary *is* the one who receives the
Gospel, St Ephrem the Syrian suggests that
one of the names of the Church is "Mary."

St Ephrem writes:

> *The Virgin Mary*
> *is a symbol of the Church,*
> > *when she receives the first*
> > *announcement of the Gospel.*
> *And, it is in the name of the Church*
> *that Mary sees the risen Jesus.*
> *Blessed be God, who filled Mary*
> *and the Church with joy.*
> *We call the Church*
> *by the name of Mary,*
> > *for she deserves a double name.*

Mary receives the announcement of the
Gospel (the "annunciation")
    and conceives the Incarnate Christ;
and it is Mary
who receives the message of the risen Lord,
    assuming, as Eve would also surely
    have thought of Adam, that he is
    "the gardener" (Jn 20.15).

Mary is the New Eve,
the obedient Virgin reversing
the disobedience of
the Virgin Eve—

and, in this way,
the true Mother of the Living,
who, as we have also seen,
is the Church.

ELEVEN

"Today you will be with me in Paradise"

We no longer know Christ in a physical body, "according to the flesh" (2 Cor 5.16).

When we finally come to "see" him,
it is as he passes out of this world.
As such, we do not now live by sight,
but by faith (2 Cor 5.7),

faith in the one who has
conquered death and is seated at the right
hand of the God and Father.

We wait in anticipation of his coming,
striving forwards
                    to meet the coming one.

And we do this knowing that in his coming,
we will be conformed to his image,
        with our bodies transformed to
        the stature of his glorious body
        (Phil 3.20–1).

And, furthermore,
this is already happening
        in those who confess their faith
            in baptism and take up the cross,
            in anticipation of the resurrection.

In all this, there is, as it were,
        a "reciprocating exodus":
to the extent that we follow Christ
in his own passage, his exodus
        or his transitus,

he returns in us.

As the Baptist said, "I must decrease so that
he might increase" (Jn 3.30).

    to the point that we can say with
the Apostle Paul:

        it is no longer I who live,
        but Christ who lives in me (Gal 2.20).

Rather than thinking of the Incarnation of
Christ as an event restricted to a long-gone
past and a far-removed land,

we should instead think of it as
a possibility that is to be lived as an
ever-contemporary reality,
here and now

    in those who respond to him.

As Israel leaving Egypt
(the Biblical image of a world
hostile to the God of Israel),
sacrificing the lamb, passing
through the waters, entering
the desert, being nourished by
manna, and journeying to the
promised land—

    we now follow Christ
by leaving the "Egypt"
of this world,

    through baptism,
    nourished by
    the Eucharist,
striving to enter into the promised land.

It was while encamping in the desert
that Israel prepared a tabernacle in which
        the Lord could "dwell."

And when it was completed, the Glory of the
Lord filled that tabernacle (Ex 40.34), as it
also later came to fill the Temple (1 Kgs 8.11).

Miniature from the illuminated
Psalter of Paris: The Crossing
of the Red Sea (10th century).

As the Epistle to the Hebrews
tells us, this was a sketch,
a preliminary model of the
reality that was enacted in,
    through, and by Christ.

He is the high priest
    of the good things
    that have come.
He entered
    through the greater and
    more-perfect tabernacle,
    not made by hands,
entering once and for all
    into the Holy Place
    by offering his own blood
and so securing an eternal redemption
(Heb 9.11–12).

So, now, those who dwell
in this world as in a desert,
    themselves become the
    temple of God,

the temple in which the Spirit dwells,
    making present throughout
    the world the glory of God:

living human beings.

Leaving this world as "Egypt"
    and dwelling in this world
    as a desert,
        we return to this world
        as Eden.

*Taking up the cross does not
    mean becoming "other-worldly,"*

for Christ comes to bring us life
and life in abundance.

But as we have seen, neither is this life
simply an affirmation of all things natural,
"all that it is to be alive."

Opposite:
Lisabeth Zwerger,
"The New Jerusalem"
(2002).

Rather, it is we, in Adam, who must say
"Let it be!"

to become, in Christ,
living human beings

—the glory of God!
And in so doing,
we discover that the Tree of Life planted
in the center of Eden is, in fact,
the cross
and that by this cross,
we come to dwell in God's paradise.

Our journey through this world,
dying to this world as "Egypt,"
through baptism, then
dying as we sojourn in the
desert of this world
by taking up the cross daily,
refashions us as living human beings,

human beings living in this world
    as God's paradise
    at the center of which stands
    the cross, the tree of life.

"Truly I say to you,
        today you will be with me
            in Paradise,"

says Christ to
the one willing to
be crucified with him
(Luke 23.43).

Are we ready,
now, to live?

REFERENCES

p. 1

St Irenaeus of Lyons, *Against the Heresies*, 4.20.7. Ed. & French trans. A. Rousseau, B. Hemmerdinger, L. Doutreleau & C. Mercier, Sources Chrétiennes 100 (Paris: Cerf, 1965); English trans. Ante-Nicene Fathers 1 (1885; repr. Grand Rapids, Mich.: Eerdmans, 1987).

p. 3

St Ignatius of Antioch, *Letter to the Romans*, 6. Ed. & trans. Ed. & trans. K. Lake, Loeb Classical Library, Apostolic Fathers 1 (Cambridge, MA: Harvard University Press, 1985 [1912]).

p. 5

St Ignatius of Antioch, *Letter to the Romans*, 3.

p. 13

St Augustine of Hippo, *Confessions*, 11.4. Trans. M. Boulding, The Works of Augustine Translated for the 21st Century 1/1 (Hyde Park, NY: New City Press, 1997).

p. 17

Origen, *Commentary on the Gospel of John*, 1.33. Ed. & French trans. C. Blanc, Sources Chrétiennes 290 (Paris: Cerf, 1982); Eng. trans. in R. E. Heine, Fathers of the Church 89 (Washington, DC: Catholic University of America Press, 1993).

p. 21

Paschal Troparion. Greek text & English translation (modified), N. M. Vaporis, *The Services for Holy Week and Easter* (Brookline MA: Holy Cross Orthodox Press, 1993).

p. 24

Paschal Homily of St John Chrysostom. Greek text & English translation (modified), Vaporis, *The Services for Holy Week and Easter*.

p. 24

"Without confusion, change, division, separation" from the Definition of the Council of Chalcedon: Trans. R. Price & M.

Gaddis, *The Acts of Chalcedon*, TTH
45, 3 vols. (Liverpool: Liverpool
University Press, 2005).

p. 27

The phrase "In the night …"
occurs in the Anaphora in the
Liturgy of St John Chrysostom.
Greek & English trans. E. Lash
(Chipping Norton, UK: Greek
Orthodox Archdiocese of Thyateira
& Great Britain, 2011).

p. 31

St Irenaeus of Lyons, *Against the
Heresies*, 5.15.2. Ed. & French trans.
A. Rousseau, L. Doutreleau & C.
Mercier Sources Chrétiennes 152–3
(Paris: Cerf, 1969); English trans. in
Ante-Nicene Fathers 1.

pp. 36–7

Nicholas Cabasilas, *The Life in
Christ*, 6.91–4. Ed. & French trans.
M.-H. Congourdeau, Sources
Chrétiennes 361 (Paris: Cerf, 1990);
English trans. C. J. deCatanzaro
(Crestwood, NY: St Vladimir's
Seminary Press, 1974), where it is
numbered as 6.12.

p. 36

Doxastikon at Vespers, Holy
Saturday. Greek & English text
(modified), Vaporis, *The Services
for Holy Week and Easter*.

pp. 37, 39

St Maximus the Confessor,
Ambigua, 41. Greek text in Patrolo-
gia Graeca 91:1309cd; English trans.
in A. Louth, *Maximus the Confessor*,
The Early Church Fathers (London:
Routledge, 1996).

p. 47

Sticheron from the aposticha,
Vespers for Saturday, tone 8.
Parakletike (Athens: 1959), attrib-
uted to St John of Damascus, &
also used in the funeral service.

pp. 49–52

St Maximus the Confessor,
Questions to Thalassius, 61. Ed. C.
Laga & C. Steel, Corpus Christiano-
rum Series Graeca 22 (Turnhout:
Brepols, 1990); Eng. trans. in P. M.
Blowers & R. L. Wilken, *On the
Cosmic Mystery of Jesus Christ:
Selected writings from St Maximus*

the Confessor, Popular Patristics Series 25 (Crestwood NY: St Vladimir's Seminary Press, 2003).

p. 54

St Irenaeus of Lyons, *Against the Heresies*, 3.24.1. Ed. & French trans. A. Rousseau & L. Doutreleau, Sources Chrétiennes 210–11 (Paris: Cerf, 1974); English trans. in Ante-Nicene Fathers 1, also in D. J. Unger & I. M. C. Steenberg, Ancient Christian Writers 64 (New York/Mahwah NJ: Paulist Press, 2012).

pp. 58–61

St Irenaeus of Lyons, *Against the Heresies*, 4.37–39.

pp. 61–4

St Irenaeus of Lyons, *Against the Heresies*, 3.20 (on Jonah); 4.39.1 ("we kill the human being in us").

pp. 69–70

St Irenaeus of Lyons, *Against the Heresies*, 5.2.3.

p. 69

St Ignatius of Antioch, *Letter to the Romans*, 4.

p. 71

Barnabas, *Letter*, 6.9. Ed. & trans. K. Lake, Loeb Classical Library, Apostolic Fathers 2 (Cambridge, MA: Harvard University Press, 1976 [1913]).

p. 75

St Maximus the Confessor, *Questions to Thalassius*, 61, & *Ambiguum* 42. Greek text in Patrologia Graeca 91:1316a–1349a; Blowers & Wilken, *On the Cosmic Mystery of Jesus Christ.*

p. 77

St Athanasius the Great, *Life of St Anthony*, 47. Ed. & French trans., G. J. M. Bartelink, Sources Chrétiennes 400 (Paris: Cerf, 1994). Trans. R. C. Gregg, *Athanasius: The Life of Antony and The Letter to Marcellinus*, Classics of Western Spirituality (New York: Paulist Press, 1980).

pp. 81–2

St Maximus the Confessor, *Ambigua*, 41.

p. 82

Dionysius the Areopagite, *On the Divine Names*, 4.13. Greek text ed. B. R. Suchla, *Corpus Dionysiacum I*, Patristische Texte und Studien 33 (Berlin: Walter de Gruyter, 1990); English trans. P. Rorem, *Pseudo-Dionysius: The Complete Works*, Classics of Western Spirituality (Mahwah, NJ: Paulist Press, 1987).

p. 87

Tertullian, *On the Soul*, 43.10. Ed. J. H. Waszink (Amsterdam: North Holland Publishing Company, 1947); English trans. in Ante-Nicene Fathers 3.

p. 88

Clement of Rome, *Second Letter of Clement*, 14. Ed. & trans. K. Lake, Loeb Classical Library, Apostolic Fathers 1 (Cambridge, MA: Harvard University Press, 1985 [1912]).

p. 89

The "Exsultet" was traditionally ascribed to St Augustine but now generally ascribed to St Ambrose. F. Brittain, ed. *The Penguin Book of Latin Verse* (Baltimore: Penguin, 1962), 94.

p. 91

Hippolytus, *On Christ and the Antichrist*, 61. Ed. H. Achelis, Die griechischen christlichen Schrift-steller der ersten drei Jahrhunderte 1.2 (Leipzig: Hinrichs Verlag, 1987); English trans. in Ante-Nicene Fathers 5.

pp. 92–7

The description of Blandina is given in *The Letter of the Martyrs of Vienne and Lyons* (probably by St Irenaeus), preserved in Eusebius, *Ecclesiastical History*, 5.1–2. Ed. & trans. K. Lake, Lobe Classical Library (Cambridge, MA: Harvard University Press, 1980 [1926]).

p. 93

St Irenaeus of Lyons, *Against the Heresies*, 5.9.2.

p. 96

St Cyprian of Carthage, *On the Unity of the Church*, 6. Ed. & trans. M. Bévenot, OECT (Oxford: Clarendon Press, 1971).

p. 99

St Ephrem of Syria, *Homily on the Night of the Lord's Resurrection*, in Thomas Josephus Lamy ed., *Sancti Ephraem Syri: Hymni et Sermones* (Mechliniae, 1882), vol. 1, p.534; trans. in L. Gambero, *Mary and the Fathers of the Church: The Blessed Virgin Mary In Patristic Thought*, trans. T. Buffer (San Francisco: Ignatius Press, 1999), 115.

p. 103

Didymus the Blind, *The Commentary on Zechariah*, 1.12–14. Ed. & French trans. L. Doutreleau, Sources Chrétiennes 83 (Paris: Cerf, 1962); English trans. R.C. Hill, Fathers of the Church 111 (Washington, DC: Catholic University of America Press, 2006).

IMAGES

Dust jacket
  Wiliam Blake, "The symbolic figure of the course of human history described by Virgil" (1824–1827). Pen and ink and watercolour over pencil, National Gallery of Victoria, Melbourne. Felton Bequest, 1920.

Dedication
  Three Dancing Bears.The Editorial Board of the University Society, *Boys and Girls Bookshelf* (New York, NY: The University Society, 1920). Image source, ClipArt ETC.

p. 2
  Mosaic of man being eaten by lions. Roman pavement fragment, Tunisia, North Africa (2nd century). Archaeological Museum, El-Jem, Tunisia. Gianni Dagli Orti / The Art Archive at Art Resource NY, ref. AA376478.

p. 7
  Masters from Campione, relief on pulpit depicting the denial of Saint Peter (12th–14th CE). Duomo, Modena, Italy. Scala / Art Resource NY, ref. ART342562.

p. 8
  Pietro Cavallini (c.1250–1330), detail from fresco depicting scenes from the life of Saints Peter and Andrew. S. Domenico Maggiore, Naples, Italy. Scala / Art Resource NY, ref. ART361094.

p. 10
  Ivory plaque depicting the encounter with Christ on the road to Emmaus (9th century). The Cloisters Collection, 1970 (1970.324.1). The Metropolitan Museum of Art, NY. Image copyright, The Metropolitan Museum of Art, NY. Image source, Art Resource, NY, ref. ART367343.

p. 16
  Fresco of the Last Supper, Karanlik Kilise (The Dark Church), Göreme, Cappadocia (12th century). Gianni Dagli Orti / The Art Archive at Art Resource, NY, ref. AA418140.

p. 19

From illuminated manuscript of
Beatus of Liébana, *Commentary on
the Apocalypse*: The Vision of the
Lamb surrounded by evangelists
and elders (c.950). MS.M. 644, f. 87.
The Pierpont Morgan Library, NY.
The Pierport Morgan Library / Art
Resource, NY, ref. ART108986.

p. 22

Icon of the Crucifixion, Ohrid
School (13th century). Icon Gallery,
Ohrid, Macedonia. Gianni Dagli
Orti / The Art Archive at Art
Resource, NY, ref. AA397562.

p. 25

Byzantine Resurrection. Line drawing, based on 9th century image of
the Anastasis in Reinhold Lange,
The Resurrection (Aurel Bongers
Recklinghausen, 1967), 29.

p. 27

Karapet of Altamar, manuscript
illumination: Deposition into the
tomb (15th century). MS 4837, f. 6v.
Matenadaran Library, Erevan,
Armenia. Scala / Art Resource, NY,
ref. ART313924.

p. 29

Leaf from manuscript of Beatus
of Liébana, *Commentary on the
Apocalypse* (c.1180). The Metropolitan Museum of Art, NY. Image
copyright, The Metropolitan Museum of Art, NY. Image source, Art
Resource, NY, ref. ART358134.

p. 30

Image from an illuminated
Gospels: The Healing of the Blind
Man (12th century). Codex 93.
Iberon Monastery, Mount Athos,
Greece. Erich Lessing / Art Re-
source, NY, ref. ART116313.

p. 32

Cupola mosaic of scenes from
Genesis (13th century). S. Marco,
Venice, Italy. Scala / Art Resource,
NY, ref. ART151875.

p. 38

A detail of the dead Christ from
a Byzantine Epitaphios (14th
century). Byzantine Museum,
Thessalonika, Greece. Photo
Werner Forman. Getty
Images: 152206038.

p. 43
Hildegaard of Bingen, *Scivias* (*Know the Ways of the Lord*) (1151). Image of the prophets and patriarchs (on left) and apostles and martyrs (on right). Lessing Archive, ref. 15-02-04/24.

p. 44
Icon of Saint Sisoes the Great before the tomb of Alexander the Great. Distributed by Holy Transfiguration Monastery.

p. 50
Pieter Bruegel, "The Land of Cockaigne" ("The Land of Plenty"), (1566). Alte Pinakothek, Bayerische Staatsgemaeldesammlungen, Munich, Germany. Art Resource, NY, ref. ART378341.

p. 52
Coptic icon of the Anastasis (14th century). The Church of Saint Barbara, Cairo. Gianni Dagli Orti / The Art Archive at Art Resource, NY, ref. AA401008.

p. 55
Detail from Romanesque painted ceiling depicting the Baptism of Jesus (c.1150). The Church of Saint Martin Zillis, Grisons Canton, Switzerland. Gianni Dagli Orti / The Art Archive at Art Resource, NY, ref. AA422192.

p. 57
William Blake, "Teach these Souls to Fly," *The Book of Urizen*, plate 2 (1796). Tate Gallery, London, Great Britain. Tate, London / Art Resource, NY, ref. ART64044.

p. 59
Georges de la Tour, detail from "Le nouveau-né" ("The Newborn"). Musée des Beaux Arts, Rennes, France. Gianni Dagli Orti / The Art Archive at Art Resource, NY, ref. AA371240.

p. 61
Giotto, Fresco of Jonah and the Whale (c.1305). Scrovegni Chapel, Padua, Italy. Alfredo Dagli Orti / Art Resource, NY, ref. ART435128.

p. 62

Image from Niko Chocheli, *The Book of Jonah* (Crestwood, NY: St Vladimir's Seminary Press, 2000), 15.

p. 64

Image of the Baptism of Christ. Line drawing, based on image in Günter Ristow, *The Baptism of Christ* (Aurel Bongers: London, 1967), 16.

p. 66

Mosaic of the Creation of the Stars (12th–13th century). Duomo, Monreale, Italy. Scala / Art Resource, NY, ref. ART101658.

p. 68

Edvard Munch, "By the Deathbed" (1896). Museum of Fine Arts, Budapest, Hungary. Album / Art Resource, NY, ref. alb1467898.

p. 71

Detail from illuminated manuscript of Rabanus Maurus, *De Universo*: The Creation of Adam (1028). Cod. 132, fol. 229. Library of the Abbey, Montecassino, Italy. Alfredo Dagli Orti / Art Resource, NY, ref. ART190760.

p. 74

Lucas Cranach the Elder, "Eve" (1533). Museum der Bildenden Kuenste, Leipzig, Germany. Erich Lessing / Art Resource, NY, ref. ART45780.

p. 75

Lucas Cranach the Elder, "Adam" (1533). Museum der Bildenden Kuenste, Leipzig, Germany. Erich Lessing / Art Resource, NY, ref. ART23505.

p. 77

Breviary of Love, Temptation: scenes of devils in everyday life (13th–14th century). Provençal codex by Ermengol de Béziers, folio 215V. Real biblioteca de El Escorial, San Lorenzo, Spain. Gianni Dagli Orti / The Art Archive at Art Resource, NY, ref. AA562435

p. 78

Anonymous, "Double portrait" (16th century). Photo: Thierry Le Mage. Louvre, Paris, France. RMN-Grand Palais / Art Resource, NY, ref. ART157238.

p. 80
Fresco on exterior wall of the
Chuch of Humor, Romania,
depicting the Meeting of Joachim
and Anna at the Golden Gate
(1530). Getty Images, ref. 150617611.

p. 85
Souvigny Bible, God creating Eve
from Adam's rib (12th century).
Folio 4v. Bibliothèque Municipale,
Moulins, France. Gianni Dagli Orti
/ The Art Archive at Art Resource,
NY, ref. AA384671.

p. 86
Hieronymus Bosch (c.1450–1516),
Triptych of Last Judgment, detail
on inside left wing: Christ creates
Eve while Adam sleeps. Akademie
der Bildenden Kuenste, Vienna,
Austria. Erich Lessing / Art
Resource, NY, ref. ART53315.

p. 92
Sister Joanna Reitlinger
(1898–1988), Icon of the martyr
Blandina and her life. Permission
sought.

p. 94
Icon of the Crucifixion, St Catherine's Monastery, Sinai, Egypt (8th
century). Photo by Fr Justin of St
Catherine's Monastery.

p. 97
Image from an illuminated manu-
script of the Four Gospels, "The
Virgin Orans." Ms. Garrett 6, fol.
11r. Manuscripts Division, Depart-
ment of Rare Books and Special
Collections, Princeton University
Library, Princeton, NJ.

p. 98
El Greco, "The Annunciation,"
(c.1600). Photo: Jozsa Denes. The
Museum of Fine Arts, Budapest /
Scala / Art Resource, NY, ref.
ART398968.

p. 101
Balage Balogh, "He Has Risen":
Mary Magdalen, Mary mother of
Jesus, and Mary Salome (the Three
Marys). Balage Balogh / Art
Resource, NY, ref. ART459375.

p. 105

> Miniature from the illuminated Psalter of Paris, "The crossing of the Red Sea." (10th century). Bibliothèque Nationale, Paris, France. DeA Picture Library / Art Resource, NY, ref. ART437533.

p. 106

> Lisbeth Zwerger, "The New Jerusalem." Illustrator, *Stories from the Bible* (New York: North-South Books, 2002), 157. Permission sought.

p. 109

> Leonhart Fuchs, woodcut of lime tree, from *De historia stirpium commentarii insignes* (Basil, 1542). Getty Images, ref. 80585242.

NOTES